The Old Mermaids Oracle

Also by Kim Antieau

Old Mermaids Books
The Blue Tail • *Church of the Old Mermaids* • *The First Book of Old Mermaids Tales* • *The Fish Wife* • *An Old Mermaid Journal* • *The Old Mermaids Book of Days and Nights* • *The Old Mermaids Book of Days and Nights: A Year and a Day Journal* • *The Second Book of Old Mermaids Tales*

Other Novels
Broken Moon • *Butch* • *Coyote Cowgirl* • *Deathmark* • *The Desert Siren* • *Her Frozen Wild* • *The Gaia Websters* • *Jewelweed Station* • *The Jigsaw Woman* • *Maternal Instincts* • *Mercy, Unbound* • *The Monster's Daughter* • *Queendom: Feast of the Saints* • *The Rift* • *Ruby's Imagine* • *Swans in Winter* • *Whackadoodle Times* • *Whackadoodle Times Two*

Other Nonfiction
Answering the Creative Call • *Certified: Learning to Repair Myself and the World in the Emerald City* • *Counting on Wildflowers: An Entanglement* • *The Salmon Mysteries: a Reimagining of the Eleusinian Mysteries* • *The Salmon Mysteries Workbook: Reimagining the Eleusinian Mysteries* • *Under the Tucson Moon*

Other Collections
Entangled Realities (with Mario Milosevic) • *Fun with Vic and Jane* • *Haunted* • *Tales Fabulous and Fairy* • *Trudging to Eden*

Chapbook
Blossoms

Blog
www.kimantieau.com

Photography
www.kimantieau.smugmug.com

The Old Mermaids Oracle
Kim Antieau

A Guide to the Wisdom of the Old Sea
and the New Desert

Green Snake
PUBLISHING

The Old Mermaids Oracle
by Kim Antieau

Copyright © 2018 by Kim Antieau.

ISBN-13: 978-1-949644-01-2
ISBN-10: 1-949644-01-4

All rights reserved.

www.kimantieau.com

No part of this book may be reproduced without written permission of the author.

Cover photo by Kim Antieau.
Book design by Mario Milosevic.
Symbols drawn by Rael Slick.

Published by Green Snake Publishing.
www.greensnakepublishing.com

Contents

Introduction 6

- Sister Sheila Na Giggles Mermaid 10
- Sister DeeDee Lightful Mermaid 14
- Sister Bea Wilder Mermaid 18
- Sister Lyra Musica Mermaid 22
- Sister Laughs A Lot Mermaid 26
- Sister Ursula Divine Mermaid 30
- Sister Bridget Mermaid 34
- Sister Ruby Rosarita Mermaid 38
- Sister Sophia Mermaid 42
- Sister Magdelene Mermaid 46
- Grand Mother Yemaya Mermaid 50
- Mother Star Stupendous Mermaid 54
- Sister Faye Mermaid 58

About the Author 62

Introduction

The Old Mermaids walked out of the Old Sea and into my imagination while I was at a writing retreat in the Sonoran Desert about 13 years ago, give or take. Every day I walked from the main house to this tiny building out by itself in the desert. Inside was an artist's table, a chair, and a bookcase. A few yards away, barely visible through the open top of the Dutch door, was a wash, an arroyo, a place where a river ran through now and again.

I wanted to write the female version of *The Old Man and the Sea*, a profound and simple story showing the soul of a woman. But such lofty aspirations can be paralyzing. In other words: that was no way to start out writing a novel! What I really needed was a character and a story. Fortunately, I began thinking about a woman walking in the desert picking up trash to turn into treasure. Myla Alvarez began telling me her story, and *Church of the Old Mermaids* was born.

The Old Mermaids are unlike any other characters I've written before or since. I love my other novels and characters. Butch (from *Butch*) is often carrying on some adventure in my head. Brooke McMurphy (from *Whackadoodle Times*) has much to say in my mind when someone cuts me off in traffic. And Gloria (from *The Gaia Websters*) is a strange kind of role model for me. But the Old Mermaids became special in ways that are difficult to articulate. They infuse nearly every part of my day and my life.

The world of the Old Mermaids disappeared, they were thrown ashore, and they built a new world. They didn't build their new world by being stoic or burying their heads in the proverbial sand. They dealt with their feelings, they dealt with their new environment, they kept true to who they each were individually and who they were as a community, and they carried on. I admired that. I started regularly asking myself "What Would the Old Mermaids Do?" The Old Mermaids Oracle evolved from that question.

This is the guidebook to that oracle. You can easily make your own pieces to represent the Old Mermaids to use with this guidebook. Choose 13 rocks you like and paint the symbols on them. (The symbols are just the initials of the Old Mermaids, so you can represent them any way you like.) Pick 13 sea shells you admire and paint them. Slice up a downed tree branch and use a wood burner to create the symbols. If you work with clay, you can easily create your set of The Old Mermaids Oracle with clay. If you are partial to cards, make cards that represent each Old Mermaid. It's fun to make little collages for each Old Mermaid.

Whatever method you pick, create the symbols with intention. Perform a ceremony or ritual when you are finished to infuse the pieces with your intentions for your Old Mermaids Oracle. Perhaps you can dip them in water for the blessing of the water, run them through a flame for the blessing of fire, breathe on them for the blessing of air, and rest them on the earth or a large piece of quartz for the blessing of earth. Once they rest on the earth, ask for the blessings of the 13 Old Mermaids.

Whichever materials you choose, I believe you will discover their connection to the Old Mermaids. Maybe that stone was one the Old Mermaids brought with them from the Old Sea. Or maybe that clay was one of the treasures the Old Mermaids carried with them as the Old Sea began disappearing. Maybe those shells were part of the treasures the Old Mermaids left in the banks of the wash as the Old Sea dried up.

You can use the booklet itself as your oracle by asking a question and then flipping through the pages and stopping on an Old Mermaid.

What I do know for sure is that these oracles you create will reveal their gifts to you over time. The more you use them, the more likely those gifts will be revealed to you.

For a divination set to become powerful, in my

view, the person who uses it will determine what each piece truly means to her. I have written about each Old Mermaid here and what the Old Ems may mean when you choose a particular one, but you'll see what they mean to you over time.

I recommend you pick one a day for a time. If you like, keep notes about what the day was like. From this, you may determine what each Old Mermaid can offer to you on any given day down the road.

Another way to use The Old Mermaids Oracle is to choose three Old Ems: One represents what is affecting you from the past; the second one represents your present; the third one is about the future. This is particularly helpful if you have a problem you are working on. Choosing three that represent the past, present, and future can sometimes help clarify the problem and highlight your choices.

Have fun with them!

Blessed sea,

Kim Antieau

P.S. You are free to make sets for yourself, but you may not make sets to sell since The Old Mermaids Oracle is my intellectual property. If you want me to make a set of oracles for you or someone else, email me for a price list at tomms@oldmermaids.com. The Old Mermaids Mystery School is up and running, and you can find out more about it and other offerings at http://www.oldmermaids.com/ or http://www.kimantieau.com/

Sister Sheila Na Giggles Mermaid

Her gift to you: Guts!
Suggestion: "Get the starfish outta your eyes, sister."
Action: Speak the truth.
Similarities and connections with: the Irish Sheela na Gig.

I can't be certain, but if you've chosen Sister Sheila Na Giggles Mermaid today, you may be in for a time of frankness. Perhaps you are the one who will be frank with someone, or perhaps someone will be frank with you. It may be a time to face some tough truths about yourself. The Old Mermaids do not hide from reality or look at life through rose-colored glasses. They face the truth. This is especially true with Sister Sheila Na Giggles Mermaid. She'll often tell you the truth, with humor. Sister Sheila Na Giggles Mermaid understands life—all of it—from beginning to end. She is a trickster. She encourages you to go deep. Speak the truth to yourself and others.

Notes

Sister DeeDee Lightful Mermaid

Her gift to you: Joy.

Suggestion: "Step lightly. Dance hard. Eat your vegetables."

Action: Be full of yourself.

Similarities and connections with: the goddesses Atargatis and Cybele. (The Romans celebrated Cybele during Hilaria—the laughing days.)

I can't be certain, but if you've chosen Sister DeeDee Lightful Mermaid today, you may be gifted with joy. Sister DeeDee Lightful Mermaid finds joy in her surroundings. She loves animals. She talks to fairies. She understands the beauty of moonlight and sunlight. She encourages us to follow our tears as well as our laughter. Mostly, she is full of her own true self. She heeds the adage of the great Greek oracle Pythia: *Know thyself.* Within is where we will find the real answers.

When the Old Mermaids first came ashore, Sister DeeDee Lightful Mermaid had trouble getting her land legs. But she familiarized herself with her surroundings, she dug deep, and she discovered she was still who she was, no matter her circumstances. She came to know that it was important to be full of her true self.

Notes

Sister
Bea Wilder
Mermaid

Her gift to you: Ecstatic dance.
Suggestion: "Things change. Get over it."
Action: Go out into nature. Dance.
Similarities and connections with: all powerful Nature deities.

I can't be certain, but if you've chosen Sister Bea Wilder Mermaid today, you might be embracing your wild nature—or heading out into Nature. Embracing the wild or embracing your wild nature has nothing to do with chaos. It is about embodying that which is natural. The wild has a rhythm, has a reason for everything. Chaos is not naturally part of the wild.

By their very nature, the Old Mermaids are communal, but they're also each very different, and not all of them are particularly gregarious. Sister Bea Wilder Mermaid is actually somewhat of a loner. She can wander the Old Mermaids Sanctuary and environs by herself—and if she doesn't want to be seen, she won't be. She often doesn't understand human social norms, but she is great at learning the rhythms of Nature. She does this by walking, walking, walking. From her connection with Nature and her knowledge of her environment, she understands that one thing remains constant: Things change.

Notes

Sister Lyra Musica Mermaid

Her gift to you: Stories.
Suggestion: "Fear has no sisters, but I have many."
Action: Sing! Play music! Focus on a goal.
Similarities and connections with: the tarot card Chariot/Hunter/Archer and Harmony of the Spheres (musica universalis), the Muses, the Pythia.

2M

I can't be certain, but if you've chosen Sister Lyra Musica Mermaid today, it might be time to find your siren song.

Sister Lyra Musica Mermaid had a difficult time when the Old Ems first came ashore. She missed the Old Sea terribly for a long time. But she forced herself to go out into Nature, she made herself face her fears, and eventually she found her siren song: her reason for being.

Perhaps it's time to "sing" your siren song, or at least begin exploring what it is. What is it in your life that brings you joy? What is it that you do well? What can you do that makes you feel as though you have found your rhythm?

Sister Lyra Musica Mermaid can help you find your rhythm, your music, your siren song—or help you focus on a goal and work toward it.

Notes

Sister Laughs A Lot Mermaid

Her gift to you: Laughter.
Suggestion: "She who laughs a lot laughs a lot."
Action: Laugh and have fun.
Similarities and connections with: Baubo, the Greek goddess who lifted her skirt and made Demeter laugh.

2A

I can't be certain, but if you've chosen Sister Laughs A Lot Mermaid today, you are in for a fun time. She is all about laughter, hugs, joy. She is sensual. She knows plants. She is happy and glittery. She is the youngest of the Old Mermaids. She will do almost anything for a laugh—as long as it's not at someone else's expense.

Laughter really can be the best medicine. When Demeter was in grief over the disappearance of her daughter, she went into a deep depression. All growth in the world stopped. But then Baubo, who is probably an ancient primordial goddess, lifted her skirt and exposed her vulva to Demeter. Demeter started laughing, and soon, her depression lifted, and it was spring again.

Sister Laughs A Lot Mermaid brings you laughter today.

Notes

Sister Ursula Divine Mermaid

Her gift to you: Knowledge of wild things.

Suggestion: "I am most at home where the wild things are."

Action: Talk to a tree or a bear today.

Similarities and connections with: Artio, Celtic bear goddess.

I can't be certain, but if you've chosen Sister Ursula Divine Mermaid, you may feel the call of the wild today.

When Sister Ursula Divine Mermaid first came to the New Desert, she had a different name. She did not immediately connect to the New Desert. Soon enough, she began hearing a call. It kept her up at night. She did not know what the call meant, or who it was for, but she had to follow it to the source. She went up into the mountains and connected with the Wild, particularly with Bear and an Old Sycamore tree who helped her get grounded and find her roots. "You are here," Old Sycamore said, and Sister Ursula Divine Mermaid finally understood the truth of it.

Sister Ursula Divine Mermaid reminds us that we are here, now, and we can root ourselves in the here and now by connecting with Nature and the wild things.

Notes

Sister Bridget Mermaid

Her gift to you: Poetry and music.
Suggestion: "Sing, dance, create. If you have to choose, do all three at once."
Action: Do something creative.
Similarities and connections with: the goddess Bridget.

I can't be certain, but if you've chosen Sister Bridget Mermaid today, you may be in store for some healing or a burst of creativity. All kinds of good things could be coming your way. Along with Sister Faye Mermaid, she is a very witchy Old Mermaid.

Sister Bridget Mermaid knows all about nearly everything: poetry, herbs, plants, songs, enchantments. Perhaps today a poem, herb, plant, or song will come your way and give you just the healing you need. She reminds us to whistle for our friends especially when we have been feeling solitary for an extended period of time.

Notes

Sister Ruby Rosarita Mermaid

Her gift to you: Enough to eat.

Suggestion: "A good bean is hard to find. Everything else is easy."

Action: Eat something wonderful and healing today.

Similarities and connections with: Gaia and Annapurna and all the goddesses of food and nourishment.

I can't be certain, but if you picked Sister Ruby Rosarita Mermaid today, be prepared for some nourishment from the Old Sea—or your kitchen.

Sister Ruby Rosarita Mermaid adjusted to the New Desert almost immediately. She loved it! She was born to cook, to feed people, to bring nourishment to all those she loved—and that was pretty much everyone. In the Old Sea, she couldn't do any of that. But in the New Desert, she flourished.

She is able to be in the moment as she gathers the materials for her enchanting dishes—including her famous storytelling soup. She talks to the plants as she harvests them. She says the best spice of all is happenstance.

Perhaps today is the day you get all the nourishment you need.

Notes

Sister Sophia Mermaid

Her gift to you: Wisdom.
Suggestion: "Go with the flow—and watch out for waterfalls."
Action: Spread some wisdom today.
Similarities and connections with: Sophia, goddess of wisdom.

S

I can't be certain, but if you've chosen Sister Sophia Mermaid today, it means you are a very wise person. Or maybe you'll be wise today—or someone will share wisdom with you.

Sister Sophia Mermaid is the distributor of cranky wisdom, often at the Tea Shell. She sees things others don't. She honors the Invisibles. She immediately saw the value and "holiness" of the New Desert. She goes with the flow, and encourages others to do the same, but like all the Old Mermaids, she understands one must keep one's eyes open. No rose-colored glasses allowed!

Notes

Sister Magdelene Mermaid

Her gift to you: Love.
Suggestion: "You ask me to tell you about love. Showing is so much better."
Action: Accept some sugar from the Universe.
Similarities and connections with: Mary Magdalene, Aphrodite, and Mary as goddess.

I can't be certain, but if you've chosen Sissy Maggie today, you are in for a whole lot of love.

Sister Magdelene Mermaid had fun at the Old Mermaids Sanctuary. And she loved everything and everyone. For her, "love" is an action verb. She demonstrated her love for the Old Mermaids, their neighbors, the Moon, the Ancestors—everything—all day by treating herself and others kindly, respectfully, and joyfully.

She made all the clothes for the Old Ems, something new for them, and she sewed enchantments, blessings, and good wishes into every piece of fabric. This was her art.

She helped build the house, plant and grow the garden, and serve others at the Tea Shell. She did all of this with enthusiasm and confidence in herself.

Perhaps today, you can grow that kind of confidence in yourself and love, love, love yourself and the rest of the world.

Notes

Grand Mother Yemaya Mermaid

Her gift to you: Mysteries of the Old Sea.
Suggestion: "Laugh or weep. We swim in your tears."
Action: Honor the Old Sea or any waterway.
Similarities and connections with: the goddess Yemaya (and every grandmother everywhere).

GM

I can't be certain, but if you've chosen Grand Mother Yemaya Mermaid today, you are in for a treat. Keep your senses open because her gift to you today can be subtle or like a tidal wave.

Grand Mother Yemaya Mermaid knows nearly everything, especially everything about the Old Ems and the Mysteries of the Old Sea. If you sit quietly with yourself, eyes closed, you may see the glint of her two tails in your imagination. She knows all, she is all. She made the quilts for the Old Mermaids, quilts created from objects she found in Nature and then sewed together with whispered enchantments and other magic.

She encourages you to go forth and protect and nurture that which needs protection and nurturing. She knows you are capable.

Notes

Mother Star Stupendous Mermaid

Her gift to you: The stars, earth, moon, and sun.
Suggestion: "All the wisdom of the ages can be distilled into one suggestion: Be."
Action: Meditate.
Similarities and connections with: the goddess Astarte.

MS

I can't be certain, but if you have chosen Mother Star Stupendous Mermaid, you will have a steady hand on your shoulder all day long.

Grand Mother Yemaya Mermaid and Mother Star Stupendous Mermaid are definitely the anchors of the Old Ems. From them, steadiness flows. The other Old Mermaids and their neighbors often come to these two when they need an answer to a question. Mother Star Stupendous is steady and calm, yet she has an eye to the stars. She definitely honors the cosmos. You can ask her a question and then meditate on it and see what will be.

Notes

Sister Faye Mermaid

Her gift to you: Healing and magic.
Suggestion: "The rest is . . . mystery."
Action: Create magic today.
Similarities and connections with: the goddess Morrigan, Morgan Le Faye, and witches.

F

I can't be certain, but if you have chosen Sister Faye Mermaid today, you are in for an injection of power into your life.

Sister Faye Mermaid, like Sister Bridget Mermaid, brought all of her skills and knowledge from the Old Sea with her to the New Desert. She knows power sea chanties (which are actually enchantments), spells, and recipes for magic pouches. She knows what ingredients to mix together with which plants to facilitate healing. She honors the plants, the environment, the Ancestors, and the Invisibles. She knows how to make things happen. She knows the magic of the desert and how to design the best ceremonies. She can get things accomplished—and so can you.

Notes

About the Author

Kim Antieau lives and writes in the Pacific Northwest. Her novels include *The Jigsaw Woman, Butch, Queendom: Feast of the Saints, Maternal Instincts*, and many others.

Kim is the creator and "guide on the side" of The Old Mermaids Mystery School and the upcoming The Old Mermaids School of Everything, and The Old Mermaids Book of Dreams. More about that here: http://www.oldmermaids.com/.

Kim's nonfiction includes *The Salmon Mysteries: A Guidebook to a Reimagining of the Eleusinian Mysteries, Under the Tucson Moon*, and *Answering the Creative Call*. Learn more at www.kimantieau.com.

Kim is also an accomplished photographer. View her photos at kimantieau.smugmug.com.

About The Old Mermaids Mystery School

Are you feeling overloaded? Surrounded by chaos? Or maybe you're no longer sure what your purpose is. Perhaps you've never known. Perhaps every once in a while you hear a whisper or a heartbeat—something—and you're certain there is more to everything. Maybe you've heard of the Church of the Old Mermaids and the Old Mermaids Sanctuary and you wonder if you could find refuge with the Old Mermaids and learn their ways.

You can.

Now their unique, practical, mystical, and poetic ways of being in and connecting with the world have been codified into The Old Mermaids Mystery School, a 13-month self-directed program to help you explore ways to swim, walk, and dance with beauty, joy, and authenticity through all the days and nights of your life. http://www.oldmermaids.com/

www.ingramcontent.com/pod-product-compliance
Lightning Source LLC
Chambersburg PA
CBHW030104100526
44591CB00008B/262